KINGSLEY SCHOOL LIBRARY

W9-AHC-665

WITHDRAWN

Kwanzaa Crafts

Evanston Public Libraries
District No. 65
Evanston, Illinois

Kwanzaa Crafts

★ A Holiday Craft Book ★

★ Judith Hoffman Corwin ★

FRANKLIN WATTS

New York ★ Chicago ★ London ★ Toronto ★ Sydney

★ **Also by Judith Hoffman Corwin** ★

African Crafts
Asian Crafts
Latin American and Caribbean Crafts

Colonial American Crafts: The Home
Colonial American Crafts: The School
Colonial American Crafts: The Village

Easter Crafts
Halloween Crafts
Thanksgiving Crafts
Valentine Crafts

Papercrafts

Forthcoming Books

Christmas Crafts
Hanukkah

★ **For Jules Arthur and Oliver Jamie** ★

Library of Congress Cataloging-in-Publication Data

Corwin, Judith Hoffman.
    Kwanzaa crafts / Judith Hoffman Corwin.
      p.   cm. — (A Holiday craft book)
    Includes index.
    ISBN 0-531-11210-1 (lib. bdg.)—ISBN 0-531-15735-0 (pbk.)
    1. Kwanzaa decorations—Juvenile literature.   2. Handicraft—
Juvenile literature.   3. Kwanzaa—Juvenile literature.   4. Afro-
Americans—Social life and customs—Juvenile literature.
[1. Kwanzaa.   2. Kwanzaa decorations.   3. Handicraft.]   I. Title.
II. Series: Corwin, Judith Hoffman.   Holiday crafts.
TT900.K92C67   1995
745.594′1—dc20
                                    94-43160
                                    CIP   AC

Contents

About Kwanzaa

Kwanzaa is an African-inspired holiday millions of African-American families celebrate from December 26 to January 1. It is a time when African Americans think back on the past year and celebrate their rich cultural history.

The holiday was started in 1966 by Maulana Karenga, Ph.D., a professor of black studies at the California State University at Long Beach, and executive director of the Institute of Pan-African Studies. All over Africa, since ancient times, people have joined together to celebrate the end of the harvest and the beginning of the new planting season. Dr. Karenga drew from the customs and rituals of several African harvest festivals to create this special holiday. It is not a religious holiday, but a celebration of African-inspired culture, and it honors the values and richness of African Americans' heritage.

Kwanza means "first" in Swahili, a language spoken in many African countries. The holiday, Kwanzaa, celebrates the "first fruits" of the harvest. There are seven letters in the word Kwanzaa, one for each of the seven principles (described on the following pages) that are the basis of the holiday. There are also seven symbols for Kwanzaa (described on pages 10–18), and the holiday lasts seven days and nights.

Each night, a table is set with the seven symbols. The family gathers as candles are lit. Thoughts are shared, stories are told, and plans are made. On the last night, a *karamu*, or glorious feast, is shared with family and friends and everyone is thankful for the joy the holiday has brought to the home.★

NGUZO SABA—The Seven Principles of Kwanzaa
by Maulana Karenga★

Every night of Kwanzaa, a family member lights a candle to celebrate one of the seven principles, nguzo saba (en-**goo**-zo sah-bah). Each principle is expressed in a Swahili word.

1. Umoja (oo-**moh**-jah)—Unity
To strive for and maintain unity in the family, community, nation, and race.

2. Kujichagulia (**koo**-gee-**cha**-goo-**lee**-ah)—Self-determination
To define ourselves, name ourselves, create for ourselves, and speak for ourselves instead of being defined, named, created for, and spoken for by others.

3. Ujima (oo-**gee**-mah)—Collective Work and Responsibility
To build and maintain our community together and make our sisters' and brothers' problems our problems and to solve them together.

4. Ujamaa (oo-**jah**-mah)—Cooperative Economics
To build and maintain our own stores, shops, and other businesses and to profit from them together.

5. Nia (**nee**-ah)—Purpose
To make our collective vocation the building and developing of our community in order to restore our people to their traditional greatness.

6. Kuumba (koo-**oom**-bah)—Creativity
To do always as much as we can, in the way we can, in order to leave our community more beautiful and beneficial than we inherited it.

7. Imani (ee-**mon**-ee)—Faith
To believe with all our heart in our people, our parents, our teachers, our leaders, and the righteousness and victory of our struggle.★

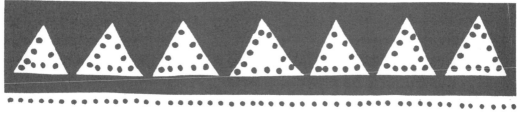

Let's Get Started

This book tells you about the Kwanzaa holiday, its history, and its meaning. It is full of ideas for making decorations, presents, wrapping paper, wonderful things to eat, and other ways to celebrate the holiday. Often, you will be able to make everything yourself, using everyday household supplies and objects. Sometimes you will need an adult to help with one or two steps in a project.

Directions for some projects include patterns for you to use to make a copy of what is shown. You don't want to cut up this book, so make a copy of the pattern with tracing paper. Begin by placing a piece of tracing paper over the pattern in the book. Using a pencil with a soft lead, trace the outline of the pattern. Turn the paper over and rub all over the pattern with the pencil. Turn it over again, and tape or hold it down carefully on the paper or fabric you have chosen to work with. Draw over your original lines, pressing hard on the pencil. Lift the tracing paper pattern and you are ready to go on with the instructions for the project.★

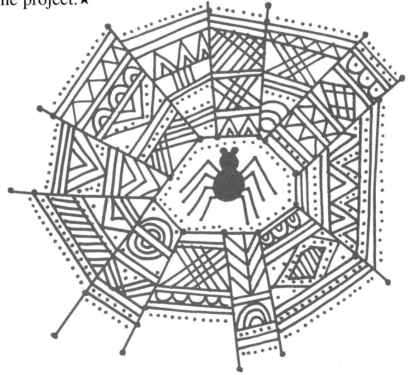

The Seven Symbols of Kwanzaa

Just as there are seven principles of Kwanzaa, there are seven Kwanzaa symbols that families display during the celebration. We will make a project for each symbol. The symbols have Swahili names.

MAZAO: CROPS★

Miniature Fruits and Vegetables

When the farm crops are ripe, everyone works together to bring in the harvest. The fruits of the harvest, the mazao (mah-**zah**-o), stand for the roots of the Kwanzaa celebration. We will make small clay fruits and vegetables to place on the Kwanzaa table.

HERE'S WHAT YOU WILL NEED★

batch of kitchen clay (recipe on page 19)
aluminum foil, paintbrushes, acrylic or poster paints, felt-tip markers
clear nail polish

HERE'S HOW TO DO IT★

1. Pull off pieces of clay and shape them into apples, pears, tomatoes, peppers, and other fruits and vegetables. Look at the illustrations here for some ideas.

2. Bake or air-dry them following the directions on page 19.

3. Use paint or markers to color and decorate the fruits and vegetables.

4. When your work is dry, seal the colors with a coat of clear nail polish.★

MKEKA: PLACE MAT★

A Kwanzaa Place Mat

Mkeka (em-**kay**-kah) is the mat upon which the other symbols may be placed. It is a symbol of tradition. An African proverb says: "If you know the beginning well, the end will not trouble you." We must pay attention to history and tradition as they are the foundation for knowledge and understanding.

HERE'S WHAT YOU WILL NEED★

newspaper
a rectangular piece of muslin, 11″ × 17″ (or longer),
   or other light-colored fabric
felt-tip or fabric markers, or acrylic paints or crayons

HERE'S HOW TO DO IT★

1. Spread newspaper over your work surface to protect it.

2. Select designs and patterns from those on pages 20–25, or plan your own designs, and use them to decorate the fabric. Use bright colors, the bolder the better.★

KINARA: THE CANDLEHOLDER★

A Kwanzaa Candleholder

The simple Kwanzaa candleholder has seven places, to hold seven candles, one for each day of the celebration. The kinara (kee-**nah**-rah) is a symbol of the African people, the ancestors of African Americans.

HERE'S WHAT YOU WILL NEED★

a scrap of wood or heavy cardboard about 8½″ × 2″
white glue
red, black, or green paint and a paintbrush
7 plastic or metal bottle caps

HERE'S HOW TO DO IT★

1. The wood or cardboard will be the base of the candleholder. Paint it and let it dry.

2. Space the seven bottle caps along the base. Check the illustration for proper placement. Glue them on. The bottle caps will serve as small cups to hold the candles.★

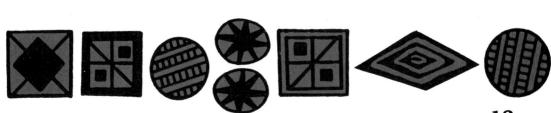

VIBUNZI: EARS OF CORN★

Miniature Ears of Corn

Vibunzi (vi-**bun**-zee), the dry ears of corn, are symbols of the family's children—one for each child. As the corn ears represent the children, the children stand for the hope of the future.

HERE'S WHAT YOU WILL NEED★

a batch of kitchen clay (see page 19)
aluminum foil
paintbrush
acrylic or poster paints, felt-tip markers
clear nail polish

HERE'S HOW TO DO IT★

1. Pull off pieces of clay and shape them into ears of corn. Check the illustration or design your own. The illustration shows an ear about 6 inches long. You can make yours that size, or make tiny ones, about 2 inches long. Remember to make one for each child in the family.

2. Bake or air-dry the corn ears.

3. Paint the kernels (you can choose to make them yellow, or multicolored, like the corn we call Indian corn) and the husks.

4. When the paint is dry, seal it with a coat of clear nail polish.★

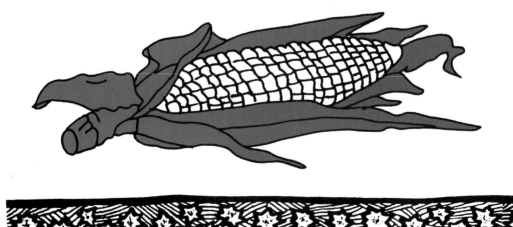

ZAWADI: GIFTS★

African Trade Beads for a Simple Gift

Zawadi (zah-**wah**-dee) are simple gifts parents give their children as rewards for their work and for their attention to the principles of Kwanzaa during the year. The gifts are usually educational (such as books) or useful, or African in spirit. Handmade gifts are the most treasured. You might like to try making Kwanzaa gifts, such as the Kwanzaa cookies (page 37), an elephant or a giraffe bank (pages 32–34), a bookmark with an African design, or this trade-bead necklace. (Directions are on the next page.)

African trade beads are treasured for their age, design, and magical powers. The tradition of making these beads from glass, shell, ivory, wood, and other materials has come down to the present day. Lovely beads can be made with kitchen clay, decorated with different colors and patterns.

HERE'S WHAT YOU WILL NEED★

a batch of kitchen clay
toothpick
cookie sheet, aluminum foil
pot holders
gold and silver paint markers
heavy thread or colored string
white, yellow, orange, red, blue, green, brown,
    and black acrylic paints
clear nail polish

HERE'S HOW TO DO IT★

1.   Read through the directions on page 19 for kitchen clay. Assemble the ingredients and make the clay. To make beads, form small balls of clay. They should be ½ inch to 1 inch high. Experiment making the different shapes and sizes shown in the illustration. You will need about twenty beads for each necklace.

2.   Push and gently twist the toothpick through the center of each bead to make a hole for stringing it.

3.   **Ask an adult to help you use the oven and to turn it on to 250°F.** Place the beads on a cookie sheet covered with aluminum foil and bake for about 5 minutes. The beads should turn a slightly darker color.

4.   Let the beads cool. To decorate them, paint them with the designs here, or try your own variations. If you have gold and silver paint markers you can add details to the beads, or paint some solid gold or silver. After the paint is dry, coat each bead with clear nail polish.

5.   When they are dry, string the beads on the thread and tie a double knot when the necklace is the right length for you. A 24-inch length of string will make a nice necklace that will fit easily over your head. The beads don't have to go all the way around the thread.★

KIKOMBE CHA UMOJA: The Unity Cup★

A Family Kwanzaa Cup

Everyone takes a sip from the unity cup, kikombe cha umoja (kee-**kom**-bay **cha** oo-**moh**-jah), to honor all the people who lived before them.

HERE'S WHAT YOU WILL NEED★

a clean Styrofoam or paper cup
colored paper or felt
pencil, scissors, white glue

HERE'S HOW TO DO IT★

1. Plan a decoration for the cup. The illustrations here may help you with some ideas.

2. Draw the shapes you want on the paper or felt. Cut them out.

3. Glue the paper or felt shapes around the cup. You could also draw or paint the designs on the cup if you wish.★

MISHUMAA SABA: Seven Candles★

Kwanzaa Candles

The mishumaa saba (mee-shu-**mah sah**-bah) represent the seven principles that are at the heart of the Kwanzaa celebration. The one black candle is placed in the center of the candle holder. It represents the richness of the African skin. Three red candles are placed at the left. They are reminders of past and present struggles. Three green candles placed to the right look toward a prosperous future. On the first night of Kwanzaa, the black candle is lit. On each of the following nights another candle is also lit—alternating first a red candle and then a green one. They are allowed to burn for just a short time, and then—on the last night—they all burn together.

HERE'S WHAT YOU WILL NEED★

7 dripless candles—1 black, 3 red, and 3 green
aluminum foil
black, red, and green squares of felt
scissors, glue

HERE'S HOW TO DO IT★

1. Cut a strip of black felt about 1 inch wide and long enough to go around the black candle, with a slight overlap. Glue the strip around the candle, about ½ inch up from the bottom.

2. Cut out 3 green strips and 3 red strips and glue them around the matching green and red candles.

3. Check the illustration and wrap the bottom of each candle with a piece of aluminum foil. Place the candles in the bottle-cap holders. The foil will catch any wax drips.

CAUTION★

Do not allow the candles to burn down to the felt bands at their bases. **Ask an adult to help with the lighting of the candles.** Never leave the room while the candles are lit.★

Kitchen Clay

With simple ingredients from the kitchen, you can quickly make your own clay to shape into many wonderful things.

INGREDIENTS★

1 cup all-purpose flour
½ cup salt
¼ cup water
1 tablespoon vegetable oil

UTENSILS★

large mixing bowl
mixing spoon
measuring cups and spoons
aluminum foil

HERE'S HOW TO DO IT★

1. Put all the ingredients into the mixing bowl. Stir until everything is completely combined. Now your clay is ready to work with.

2. Follow the directions for your project (perhaps a spirit person from page 28, or use the African designs on pages 20–25, or a project you think up yourself) and shape the clay. You will now need to let your clay objects dry and get hard. You can leave them to air-dry on a piece of aluminum foil for a few days. Or you can bake them on aluminum foil in the oven, at 350°F for about 10 minutes. **Ask an adult to help you use the oven**. If the projects are larger than 3 inches, they will need a little more time in the oven. When finished, they should be hard to the touch.

3. Allow the clay to cool and then decorate it, following the instructions for your project.★

African Patterns

African patterns, designs, and images are extremely bold and expressive. They are creations of a culture in which art and design are an important part of everday life. Everyday objects are decorated in a natural way, with the designs fitting into the object's function. On the following pages, you will find a variety of designs. Experiment with them and use them on your Kwanzaa place mat (Mkeka), on Kwanzaa gifts (Zawadi), greeting cards, wrapping paper, pictures, T-shirts, and wall decorations. Let your imagination be your guide, because part of the celebration of Kwanzaa is appreciation of the creative spirit. These designs can inspire your own original drawings, too. You can draw them larger or smaller, or change them as you wish. To begin, all you need is a pencil and a piece of paper.★

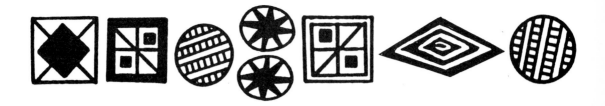

AMANI
JAMAA
SIKUKUU
UPENDO
SHIRIKIANA
MILA
HESHIMA
FURAHA
KAZI

JAMAA
MILA

SHIRIKIANA

AMANI AMANI AMANI AMANI

HESHIMA

Decorating with Swahili Words

Here are some Swahili words (along with their English meanings) that we use in talking about the Kwanzaa holiday. Try writing them in different ways, to make artworks using them. The illustrations here will give you some ideas, and then you can find your own interesting ways to write them. Make some letters larger than others, write them in a curve, up and down, sideways. Make them tall and very thin, or thick and fat. Use felt-tip markers, colored pencils, crayons, a paintbrush or even a stick dipped in paint. Try splashing some paint around the letters also. Try mixing crayons, paint, and markers to create a unique work. Use your artwork to decorate a greeting card, or wrapping paper, or stationery. Being creative and free is part of what the Kwanzaa spirit and celebration is about. Have fun.

HERE'S WHAT YOU WILL NEED★

paper, felt-tip markers, colored pencils, crayons, paints, paintbrushes envelopes, newspaper

HERE'S HOW TO DO IT★

Decide whether you want to make a greeting card, wrapping paper, or stationery. Choose paper to work on. If you are making a greeting card, fold it in half and select an envelope that it will fit into. You might have to trim the paper to make it fit. Remember to spread newspaper over your work surface to protect it.★

Swahili	English
Amani	Peace
Jamaa	Family
Sikukuu	Holiday/Celebration
Upendo	Love
Shirikiana	Sharer/Partner
Mila	Tradition
Heshima	Pride
Furaha	Happiness/Joy
Kazi	Work

Spirit People

These little spirit people appear in ancient tribal art as tiny "good-luck" tokens. They can be made to represent your spirit, or an ancestral spirit, or they can be a bit of art to wear and collect. They will carry the Kwanzaa celebration wherever you travel. They make great gifts and are fun to trade and collect. One evening, as part of a Kwanzaa celebration, everyone can make their own. A school class or a club can make them, and exhibit and talk about them when they are finished. Try using many patterns and textures on your spirit person.

28

Solve E Lawrence
District No. 65
Evanston, Illinois

HERE'S WHAT YOU WILL NEED★

1 square of felt (any color)
tracing paper, pencil, pins, scissors
white glue, safety pin
scraps of a variety of fabrics
small stones, old jewelry, buttons, beads, charms,
   feathers, bits of fur, yarn, thread, string, twigs, shells, bottle caps,
   corks, straws, plastic spoons, forks
6 to 8 cotton balls, or rags
black permanent felt-tip marker
gold or silver paint markers

HERE'S HOW TO DO IT★

1. Following the directions on page 9, make a copy of this pattern. Fold the piece of felt in half, and pin the pattern to it. Cut it out. You will have two pieces, one for the front and one for the back. Put one piece aside. Draw a thin line of glue all along the outside edge of the other piece, which will be the back.

2. Gently pull apart some of the cotton balls and place them on the felt, inside the line of glue. You won't need much, this is just to give some shape to the spirit person. If you have a good-luck charm or coin, or a secret message, tuck it inside.

3. Place the front piece on top of the back and press all along the outside edge to glue them together. You may have to add a little glue in some places. Allow this to dry.

4. From one fabric scrap, cut a small circle for the face. Draw on a nose and mouth with a marker. Draw eyes, or glue on buttons or beads for eyes. For hair, glue on strips of fabric or yarn, straw, feathers, or twigs. With yarn, thread, or fabric scraps, you can wrap your spirit person in a shirt, skirt, pants. Add shoes or a headdress, if you like. Check the illustrations for ideas, then let your imagination run wild. Attach anything that you have especially saved to add to your spirit person.★

School Libraries
Digital N...
...son Trailers

African Proverb Scroll

Here are some African proverbs that are fun to read and think about. Try writing some on this simple scroll and you can bring it out to share with a friend, or read in a quiet moment.

HERE'S WHAT YOU WILL NEED★

3 sheets of white typing paper, glue, black felt-tip marker
cardboard tube (from a roll of paper towels or aluminum foil)
scrap of fabric or piece of 1″-wide ribbon, 6″ long

HERE'S HOW TO DO IT★

1. Glue the 3 sheets of paper together along their long sides, to make one long piece of paper for the scroll. Choose the proverbs you would like to write on your scroll.

2. After you have filled your scroll, glue the left side to the paper tube, as shown. Allow it to dry.

3. Roll up the scroll, as shown. Tie the ribbon or scrap of fabric around the scroll to keep it from unrolling.★

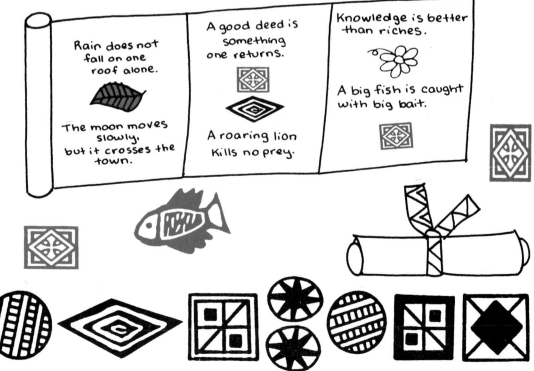

AFRICAN PROVERBS★

The cow that arrives early gets the good drinking water.
Darkness conceals the hippopotamus.
Even an ant can harm an elephant.
We start as fools and become wise through experience.
A roaring lion kills no prey.
Do not throw mud in the well as you leave your host's house.
A word spoken cannot be taken back.
To be without a friend is to be poor, indeed.
One cannot count on riches.
To try and to fail is not laziness.
In the ocean, one does not need to sow water.
If you climb up a tree, you must climb down the same tree.
A big fish is caught with big bait.
A person who is being carried does not realize how far the town is.
When the mouse laughs at the cat, there is a hole nearby.
The person who boasts much can do little.
A little rain each day will fill the rivers to overflowing.
A good deed is something one returns.
No matter how long the winter, spring is sure to follow.
The moon moves slowly, but it crosses the town.
If you do not step on a dog's tail, the dog will not bite you.
By trying often, the monkey learns to jump from the tree.
Knowledge is better than riches.
Rain does not fall on one roof alone.
The person who hunts two rats catches none.
What has been blown away cannot be found again.
The fool is thirsty in the midst of water.
The frog tried to be as big as the elephant and burst.
Unless you call out, who will open the door?
When spider webs are joined, they can tie up a lion.
No matter how long the night, the day is sure to come.
No matter how full the river, it still wants to grow.
While two birds argued over a seed, a third swooped down and carried
   it off.

African Elephant Bank

The African elephant is a symbol of power and royalty. Its image has been drawn, painted, carved, woven, and sculpted since ancient times—on both everyday and ceremonial objects. The elephant's enormous size, fanlike ears, huge ivory tusks, wrinkled hoselike trunk, small eyes, and stringy tail, make it a remarkable animal.

   We will make a bank with an elephant on it, to save money for next year's Kwanzaa celebration. The bank will be made from a 16-ounce glass jar, like one from apple sauce. Through the clear glass you will be able to see your Kwanzaa savings mount up! ★

HERE'S WHAT YOU WILL NEED★

white oaktag or cardboard
pencil, tracing paper, scissors
black fine-line marker
colored markers, or colored pencils
glue, string, gray felt, black bead or button
16-ounce glass jar, such as an apple sauce jar

HERE'S HOW TO DO IT★

1.   Clean out the empty jar. Be sure to remove the label. Follow the directions given on page 9 and copy the elephant pattern. Transfer it to the oaktag and cut it out. Go over all the lines with the black fine-line marker and then color the elephant gray. Color in the designs on the blanket. Glue the finished elephant onto the bottle, as shown. Cut a few strands of string and glue them on to make a tail, as shown.

2.   Copy the pattern for the elephant's ear on the paper. Place it on the felt and cut it out. Glue this in place, and glue on a bead or button eye, as shown.★

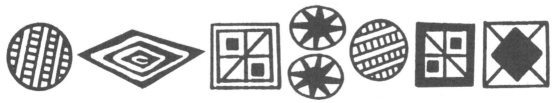

A Vegetable Garden

Kwanzaa, or "first fruits," can be expressed by creating your own little garden. A garden can be made by cutting pieces from several different fruits and vegetables that you might find in your kitchen and letting them grow roots in jars of water. Try using pieces of carrot, pineapple, sweet potato, white potato, or an avocado pit.

HERE'S WHAT YOU WILL NEED★

a carrot, pineapple, sweet potato, white potato, or avocado pit
knife, small jars or containers, water, toothpicks

HERE'S HOW TO DO IT★ Ask an adult to help you.

1. Checking the illustrations, cut off only the top of the carrot and pineapple. Slice an end piece off the sweet potato or white potato. If you are using an avocado, cut it in half and pull out the pit. Place 3 or 4 toothpicks into the piece and then put it into a container of water, so that it sits on the water. Check the illustration. The water should not be above the toothpicks; they hold the fruit or vegetable in place so that roots will begin to grow down into the water. If you use glass containers, you can see the roots grow. When the roots almost fill the container, you can move your plant to a larger container, this one with earth in it. Now you have a real plant ready to develop and grow. Remember to water it whenever the soil feels dry.★

Kwanzaa Star Game

This game looks easy, but it isn't—until you discover the trick. Try to figure out the secret yourself. If you're stuck, the answer is on the last page of this book. Once you know the trick, try the game with your family and friends at your Kwanzaa celebration.

HERE'S WHAT YOU WILL NEED★

4 pennies
sheet of 8″ × 11″ paper
pencil

HERE'S HOW TO DO IT★

1. In the center of the paper draw a star about 5 inches in size. Check the illustration to see how it should look.

2. Place the first penny on a point of the star. Move it along a straight line to reach an opposite free point.

3. Take the other three pennies, one at a time, and try to move them from any free point to another free point.

4. This game can be a good Kwanzaa present. Draw the star on a piece of paper. Write the instructions on another piece of paper. On a scrap of paper, write out the secret to the game. Fold and tape this scrap closed, and write on the outside: "Do not open until you have tried the game for half an hour."★

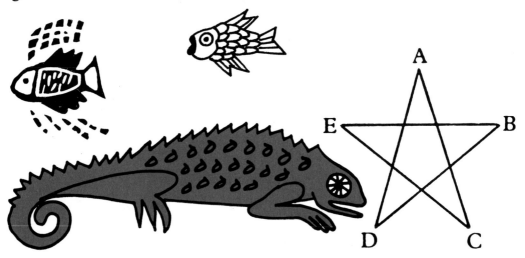

Kwanzaa Cookies

These Kwanzaa cookies are double chocolate cookies, a chocolate cookie with chocolate chips inside. They make splendid Zawadi, or simple gifts, in keeping with the tradition of making and exchanging homemade things. You can make them every year and they can become part of your family's Kwanzaa celebration.

INGREDIENTS★

1½ cups sugar
4 large eggs
16 ounces semisweet chocolate
¼ cup sweet butter, softened
1 tablespoon vanilla
1 tablespoon brewed coffee
½ cup all-purpose flour
1 teaspoon baking powder
¼ teaspoon salt
½ teaspoon cinnamon
1½ cups semisweet chocolate pieces

UTENSILS★

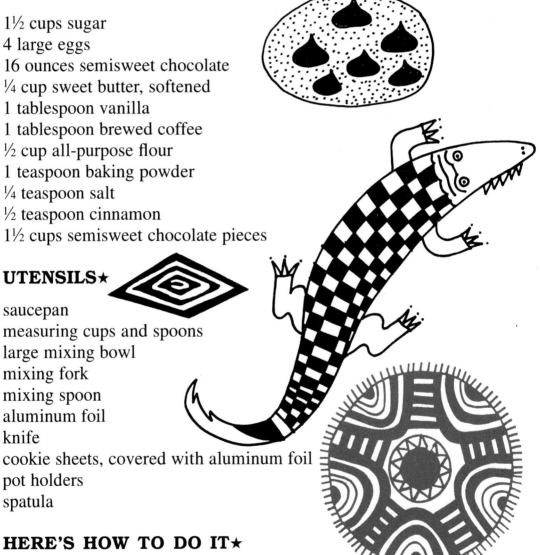

saucepan
measuring cups and spoons
large mixing bowl
mixing fork
mixing spoon
aluminum foil
knife
cookie sheets, covered with aluminum foil
pot holders
spatula

HERE'S HOW TO DO IT★

Ask an adult to help you.

1. In the saucepan, over low heat, melt the 16 ounces of chocolate. Set aside to cool.

2. In the mixing bowl, beat the sugar and butter with a fork until it is thick and lemon-colored.

3. Add the melted chocolate, butter, vanilla, coffee, flour, baking powder, salt, and cinnamon. Stir until everything is completely combined. Add the chocolate pieces.

4. On a piece of aluminum foil, form the dough into a log that is about 3 inches around. Wrap the dough in the foil and put it in the refrigerator for about an hour, until it is firm enough to cut.

5. When the dough is firm, cut it into 1-inch round slices. Place these about 1 inch apart on foil-covered cookie sheets.

6. **Ask an adult to help you use the oven.** Preheat it to 350°F. Bake the cookies for about 15 minutes, or until the tops are slightly cracked and shiny. The cookies will be soft. Allow them to cool for just a minute and then remove them with a spatula and place them on a platter. The cookies will become firm when they are cool. Makes about 15 large cookies.★

Kwanzaa Corn Muffins

Corn is one of the symbols of Kwanzaa—the ears stand for the children in the family. Corn is also an important and plentiful food. Corn muffins can be prepared quickly and are almost a meal because they contain bacon. Serve them with some butter and jam and they are sure to please. Wrapped in plastic, tied up with red and green ribbons, they make welcome Kwannzaa presents.

INGREDIENTS★

6 slices bacon
¼ cup bacon drippings
1 cup all-purpose flour
1 cup cornmeal
3 tablespoons sugar
1 tablespoon baking powder
1 cup milk
1 egg
½ cup canned corn kernels, drained

UTENSILS★

frying pan, fork
paper towels
large mixing bowl
mixing spoon
measuring cups and spoons
muffin tin
paper cupcake liners
pot holder, toothpick

HERE'S HOW TO DO IT★

1. **Ask an adult to help you fry the bacon until it is crisp.** Drain the slices and let them cool on a paper towel. Keep ¼ cup of the drippings. Crumble the bacon and set it aside on a paper towel.

2. In the mixing bowl, combine the flour, cornmeal, sugar, baking powder, and salt. Add the milk, egg, corn kernels, and bacon drippings, stirring until well blended. Add the crumbled bacon. Mix well.

3. Place the paper cupcake liners in the muffin tin. Spoon batter into each liner, filling it about two-thirds full.

4. **Ask an adult to help turn on the oven.** Preheat it to 400°F. Put the muffins into the oven and bake for about 15 minutes, or until a toothpick inserted in the center comes out clean. The tops should be slightly browned. Yield: 12 muffins.★

Peanut Butter Cookies

The peanut is native to South America and was grown there by the Indians. Early explorers carried it to Africa and it was then brought to North America in slave-trading days. Today, the peanut is a valuable crop in southern states because of its varied uses, many of which were developed by George Washington Carver, a famous African-American scientist. The seeds of the plant, the peanuts, are eaten fresh or roasted, used in cooking and in candy. They are also ground into peanut butter. Peanut oil is used for cooking, in the making of soap, and in other ways. The leaves of the plant are used to feed livestock.

These are golden brown, rich, chewy peanut butter cookies that are great to serve as a dessert at your Kwanzaa celebration. They could also be given as a present. Wrap them in plastic and cut out a fancy shape from paper or fabric and glue it onto the package. Check pages 20–25 for design ideas. You could write the recipe on a piece of paper and include it with the cookies.

INGREDIENTS★

½ cup sweet butter, softened
½ cup firmly packed brown sugar
½ cup granulated sugar
1 egg
1 cup peanut butter
½ teaspoon salt
½ teaspoon baking soda
1 teaspoon vanilla
1¼ cups all-purpose flour

UTENSILS★

measuring cups and spoons
large mixing bowl
mixing spoon and fork
cookie sheets, covered with aluminum foil
fork
pot holders
spatula

40

HERE'S HOW TO DO IT★

1. **Ask an adult to help you use the oven.** Preheat it to 350°F. In the large mixing bowl, combine the butter, brown sugar, and granulated sugar. Beat until creamy.

2. Add the egg, peanut butter, salt, baking soda, and vanilla. Stir until completely combined. Now add the flour, stirring until blended.

3. To form the cookies, take a teaspoonful of dough and form it into a ball with your hands. Place the ball on a foil-covered cookie sheet. Press a fork gently on the cookie to flatten it slightly. Repeat this for all the cookies. Bake for 10 to 12 minutes, until golden. Remove them with a spatula. Makes about 60 cookies.★

Peanut Butter Fudge

Peanut butter and chocolate chips are combined to make a quick fudge candy that can be wrapped in decorative paper and given as a Kwanzaa present.

INGREDIENTS★

2 cups sugar
⅔ cup milk
2 tablespoons light corn syrup
1 tablespoon butter
1 teaspoon vanilla
½ cup peanut butter
1 cup chocolate chips

UTENSILS★

measuring cups and spoons
medium-size saucepan
mixing spoon
glass of cold water
8″ × 8″ × 2″ pan, greased with butter
knife

HERE'S HOW TO DO IT★

1. **Ask an adult to help you use the stove.** In the saucepan, combine the sugar, milk, and corn syrup. Bring the mixture to a boil over medium-high heat, stirring constantly until mixture boils. Allow the mixture to continue to boil for about 3 to 5 minutes. To test if the mixture is cooked, drop a little from a spoon into a glass of cold water. If it forms a soft ball you know it is cooked enough. Remove it from the heat. Add the butter and allow the mixture to cool.

2. Add the vanilla and peanut butter, and beat until the mixture begins to thicken and lose its glossy look. Be careful, because this happens quickly. Add the chocolate chips and spoon into a buttered pan. While the fudge is still warm, mark it into squares. Cool until firm in the refrigerator, and then cut as marked. This makes about 36 pieces.★

A Parade of African Animals

A lion, elephant, leopard, monkey, python, zebra, crocodile, hippopotamus, giraffe, ostrich, rhinoceros, and chimpanzee are all on parade. Lines are simple, flat, expressive, and very, very bold! You can learn to draw them quickly and easily by first sketching them in pencil and then drawing over the lines with markers. Using this speedy method, you can make broad strokes that are repeated so that animals can be "built" simply. The drawings can decorate almost anything—greeting cards, stationery, wrapping paper, notebook covers, T-shirts, fabric—or you could add a house and trees and make a mural of an African scene.

HERE'S WHAT YOU WILL NEED★

white paper, pencil, felt-tip markers
colored pencils, paints, paintbrushes

HERE'S HOW TO DO IT★

Begin by looking at the drawings here and deciding which ones you want to use. All the animals are made up of simple shapes. You can make them any size you like. Don't worry about copying them exactly; that's not the point. It is important that they be expressive. After you practice a little, you will gain confidence and enjoy the results. Color the animals if you like.★

44

Index

The secret of the Kwanzaa Star Game is to move the second penny to the place where you started the first one, and so on. For example, Move A to C, D to A, B to D, and E to B.

School Libraries
Evanston, Illinois